ANNIHILATION IN AUSTIN

THE SERVANT GIRL ANNIHILATOR MURDERS OF 1885

COLD CASE CRIME SERIES #3

TIM HUDDLESTON

Absolute Crime Press

ANAHEIM, CALIFORNIA

ABSOLUTE CRIME

www.AbsoluteCrime.com

Contents

About Absolute Crime...6

Chapter 1: Bloody Work...10

Chapter 2: Reign of Terror......................................23

Chapter 3: Another Deed of Deviltry....................30

Chapter 4: The Servant Girl Annihilators...............38

Chapter 5: An Atrocious Crime 44

Chapter 6: Slain in Their Sleep..............................49

Chapter 7: The Noble Detectives..........................56

Chapter 8: Blood! Blood! Blood!...........................63

Chapter 9: Nathan Elgin.......................................72

Chapter 10: Trial of the Century...........................79

Epilogue: A Killer's Legacy....................................89

Reference..94

Ready for More? 100

Newsletter Offer...108

ABOUT ABSOLUTE CRIME

Absolute Crime publishes only the best true crime literature. Our focus is on the crimes that you've probably never heard of, but you are fascinated to read more about. With each engaging and gripping story, we try to let readers relive moments in history that some people have tried to forget.

Remember, our books are not meant for the faint at heart. We don't hold back--if a crime is bloody, we let the words splatter across the page so you can experience the crime in the most horrifying way!

If you enjoy this book, please visit our homepage (www.AbsoluteCrime.com) to see other books we offer; if you have any feedback, we'd love to hear from you!

Sign up for our mailing list, and we'll send you out a free true crime book!

http://www.absolutecrime.com/newsletter

CHAPTER 1: BLOODY WORK

December 31st, 1884

"Mr. Tom, for God's sake do something to help me! Somebody has nearly killed me!"

It was three o'clock in the morning and Walter Spencer had staggered into Tom Chalmers' bedroom, waking the seventeen-year-old from a deep sleep and scaring him half to death. Tom lit the kerosene lamp on the table next to his bed and was horrified by what the dim light revealed. Spencer had spoken true; by the look of him, he had taken the beating of his life. He had five or six deep gashes to his head, his face was swollen and disfigured as if pieces of his skull had been knocked out of place, and he was absolutely covered in blood.

Spencer was the boyfriend of Mollie Smith, the servant girl who had been working for Tom's sister and brother-in-law, Mr. and Mrs. William K. Hall, for the past month or so. The two of them lived together as common-law man and wife in a small apartment behind the kitchen, and neither one of them had ever been in the least bit of trouble. Tom jumped out of bed and asked Spencer what had happened to him, but the injured man was only able to mutter a stream of semi-coherent thoughts. All he claimed to know for certain was that he had woken up in his present condition and Mollie was nowhere to be found.

Tom knew Spencer to be an honest and honorable man, but he suspected that he wasn't telling the full truth. He had heard from the Halls' other servants that Mollie had a fiery spirit and a ferocious temper. Before she had come to Austin, her previous employer in Waco had walked in on her threatening to kill her former lover with a broken bottle. Tom wasn't aware of any tension between the couple, but Spencer was something of a meek man, and he had seen Mollie boss him around from time to time. He must have done something to anger the girl and she had lost control of herself and beaten him to the brink of death. Now, he was most likely lying in an effort to keep Mollie out of jail.

Tom decided that a lovers' quarrel between Negroes was none of his concern, so he told Spencer to leave his room and go to the doctor's house to get himself fixed up. Spencer asked Tom to help him get there; he was so weak that he was afraid he might not make it on his own. But Tom refused. His sister was very ill and he said he didn't feel right leaving the house in the middle of the night in case she might need him. Of course, there were other people at home, including Mr. Hall himself and Mrs. Hall's nurse, Nancy, but Walter Spencer was no fool and he knew better than to argue with a white man. He did as he was told and shuffled out of the room and out the back door of the house while Tom put out the lamp and went back to bed.

In the morning, William Hall came downstairs and found that the fires weren't lit and breakfast wasn't on the table, which was very odd indeed. As long as Mollie had been working for him she had never once been delinquent in her duties. But after learning of Tom's late-night encounter with Spencer, Mr. Hall assumed that Mollie must have left town to avoid trouble with the law, just as she had done in Waco. Apparently, the willful young woman was leaving a string of spurned lovers across the entire great state of Texas. Well, servant girls were easy enough to find. New people were arriving in Austin looking for work every day; he would have no trouble replacing her.

The rest of the morning proceeded as normal, until around nine o'clock when Mr. Hall heard shouts coming from the backyard. He rushed outside to see what was going on and found a neighbor's servant boy standing by the outhouse. The boy had seen something strange lying on the ground and had walked over to investigate. What he found had stricken him with horror.

It was Mollie Smith. The pretty, young, mixed-race girl was lying dead on the ground, her head cleaved nearly in two. Her blood had soaked into the snow around her, staining it dark red, her nightgown had been ripped to shreds, no longer covering much of anything, and her legs were spread wide. A trail led to the back door of the house, indicating that Mollie had been dragged to where she now lay, half-hidden in the tall grass behind the outhouse. Mr. Hall followed the trail to Mollie's living quarters and what he found inside the room was nearly as frightening as the sight of the dead girl herself.

The apartment had practically been re-painted with Mollie's blood. It seemed as if there was more blood in the room than could have possibly fit in the human body. There was blood on the bed, soaking the pillows, linens and mattress, there was blood on the floor, seeping into the boards, there was blood spattered all across the walls, and worst of all...there was a bloody axe at the foot of the bed. Mr. Hall wasted no time in sending for Austin's marshal, Grooms Lee.

Marshal Lee was not the most popular lawman in the state of Texas. In fact, earlier that year, he had nearly been impeached when it became known that he and the twelve officers who made up Austin's police force seemed to spend most of their time "investigating" saloons, brothels and gambling dens whether there had been any crimes reported in the area or not. At best, Lee could be described as unfit, and many suspected that he was utterly corrupt, but he was the son of a powerful local politician, so ousting him from his position had proven impossible. When it came to law enforcement, he was all the city of Austin had.

Lee had seen a murder or two in his time as marshal, but never anything like what had occurred at the Halls' residence. The brutality with which this poor colored girl had been attacked seemed inhuman. The condition of her room indicated that there had been a desperate struggle; it was clear Mollie had not gone down without a fight. Furniture had been overturned, a looking glass had been shattered and there were bloody handprints smeared across the doorframe. It seemed as though she had sustained her injuries inside the room, and was then dragged outside behind the outhouse where she was raped while dying or possibly already dead.

While examining the ruin of Mollie's body, Lee found a set of wide, bare footprints in the snow. He followed them about a block away, to the shore of Shoal Creek, where they seemed to simply disappear. He sent for the tracker, who brought his pack of bloodhounds led by the surly but trusty Old George. If there were a scent to be found, Old George would almost certainly find it. Or at least, that was all Marshal Lee could hope for. In the late nineteenth century, law enforcement had yet to develop much of anything in the way of investigative tactics. There were no blood-spatter analysts or DNA tests, and even the science of fingerprinting was still a few years from becoming common practice. Unless a crime had been witnessed or confessed to, there was little that could be done to find the culprit. The bloodhounds were essentially the only tools at Lee's disposal, and in this case, the dogs had come up empty. That left Lee with no other option but to discern motive and means.

Lee believed that the most obvious scenario was a variation of what Tom Chalmers had thought when Walter Spencer had awakened him in the small hours of the morning. Perhaps he and Mollie had gotten into an argument that had gotten out of hand. After all, Mollie's temper was well documented; maybe she hit Spencer and he had fought back and killed her. But that seemed unlikely for many reasons. First of all, by most accounts, the couple was very happy and no one had ever seen them exchange any angry words. And Walter was such a relaxed, easy-going young man, it was doubtful that he had it in him to commit such a violent act as to strike his common-law wife with an axe, much less drag her out behind the outhouse and have his way with her body before going back inside to seek help from Tom Chalmers. And where would he have gotten the axe? It didn't belong to the Halls and Walter wouldn't have had the money to buy it himself. Lee supposed it could have been stolen, but that suggested premeditation, and if Spencer were the murderer, it would surely have been a crime of passion. Furthermore, Dr. Bart, the man who treated Spencer's wounds, said that his injuries didn't come from an axe, but seemed to have been inflicted by a rod of iron or steel, and that weapon had not been found. Why would Spencer have disposed of the tool he had been attacked with, yet leave the murder weapon behind for all to see? It simply didn't add up.

Later in the afternoon, after Spencer had more or less regained his senses, Marshal Lee and the crime reporter from the Austin Daily Statesman, the local newspaper, interviewed the injured man, hoping to gain some new insight. Spencer, still in terrible pain, stated that he and Mollie had gone to bed around nine or ten in the evening. He mentioned that Mollie didn't feel well and that she had asked him to wake her early in the morning. The next thing he claimed to remember was waking up injured and finding Mollie gone, just as he had told Tom Chalmers. When asked if he knew of anyone who may have wished him and Mollie harm, the only name Spencer could come up with was William "Lem" Brooks.

Lem was Mollie's old boyfriend, the man she had nearly killed with a broken bottle back in Waco. When she had moved to Austin, he had followed her and not long ago, he had challenged Spencer to a fight. Mollie's vicious murder and rape certainly seemed as if it could be attributed to jealousy, so Marshal Lee had Brooks arrested.

Brooks may have had a solid motive, but once he was questioned, his guilt became doubtful. Lem admitted to the incident in Waco, but claimed to have no further quarrel with Mollie and denied Spencer's claims that he had wanted to fight him. He swore he was innocent and even had an alibi to back it up. Lem said he had been at a dance on Sand Hill, nearly two miles from the Halls' house on West Pecan Street, and several witnesses had seen him there as late as four o'clock in the morning, an hour after Walter Spencer had woken Tom Chalmers. But every last one of Lem's witnesses were Negroes, which made their credibility suspect at best, as far as Marshal Lee was concerned.

On New Years' Day, 1885, an inquest was held to decide if there was enough evidence to bring Brooks to trial. The six white men who made up the coroner's jury listened to witness testimony behind closed doors for four straight days. Each day, the press was denied access to the proceedings and each day, they complained about it in the papers. Clearly, the secrecy that surrounded the inquest meant that there were details of the crime that were being kept from the public at large. But wouldn't it benefit the investigation if everyone knew exactly what had occurred that horrible night? Wouldn't the perpetrator be found more easily if the whole town knew the exact truth of every clue found at the scene?

When the inquest was called to an end, no new information was presented to the public, but it was announced that William "Lem" Brooks would indeed stand trial for the murder of Mollie Smith. By the time the preliminary trial was scheduled, however, Brooks was freed due to lack of evidence. No other suspect was charged.

*   *   *

The final day of 1884 had brought with it one of the most horrible crimes Austin, Texas had ever seen. But the murder of Mollie Smith was only the beginning. Before 1885 was over, the people of Austin would find themselves in the center of a violent and terrifying mystery that would reach from the lowest of the city's lower class all the way up to its highest of high society. The capital of Texas had become the hunting ground of a terrifying new type of criminal. And although everyone who lived through the events of that year would remember them for the rest of their lives, they would be all but lost in the annals of history for over a hundred years.

CHAPTER 2: REIGN OF TERROR

At the end of the Civil War, Austin was only a rustic ranch town with a population of less than 5,000 people. But after twenty hard years of Reconstruction, the city was well on the way to becoming a bustling, modern metropolis. By 1885, the population had grown to 23,000 residents who were shuttled around their expanding city on mule-drawn streetcars. Telephone party lines crisscrossed the sky while new up-scale restaurants, opera houses, bookstores and art studios opened on a regular basis. There was even a new capitol building being

built and when completed, it would be a tower
of pink granite that would cement Austin's rep-
utation as the "Athens of the West."

Austin was expanding socially, as well. Un-
like many southern cities in the post-war era,
Austin was known for being reasonably accom-
modating towards its black population. Former
governor E.M. Pease had donated several
acres of land to his own freed slaves, creating
Clarksville, Austin's second black neighborhood. One of the city's three colleges, Tillotson
Collegiate and Normal Institute, was opened
specifically to educate black students. And
while racial segregation was the norm, there
were African-American entrepreneurs who
owned businesses on the almost entirely white
Pecan Street. Austin was a progressive city and
one that was growing very fast. Maybe it was
fair to say that it was growing too fast for its
own good.

Following the murder of Mollie Smith, Austin saw an epidemic of serious and often violent crimes being perpetrated against
domestics. Night after night, servants' quarters
were broken into and robbed. Rocks were

thrown through windows, death threats were shouted, and in the worst cases, women were beaten and raped (or "outraged" to use the terminology of the era). Sometimes it was a single man committing these attacks, sometimes two, sometimes a whole gang. And as the year wore on, the criminals became bolder and bolder.

On March 14th, the Statesman reported that there had been four attacks in a single night. In one instance, a gang of ruffians tried to break into the apartment of a black woman and her husband. The man had a pistol and fired at the thugs through the door, successfully scaring them off. A short time later, a lone perpetrator attempted to force his way into the room of two young servant girls, but they ran outside screaming and the neighbors came to their aid. Later that night, another woman was assaulted, but she managed to fight off her assailants before suffering serious injury. The final victim of the evening, however, wasn't so fortunate. She was attacked by two men, then held down and beaten while they forced themselves on her. While she suffered the worst of the night's attacks, she was also the only one who was able to identify the men who had harmed her. She told police that one of the two men was a mixed-race barber named Abe Pearson who had painted his skin with lamp-black to appear darker. Pearson was arrested and the woman testified to his identity, making him the only perpetrator of any of these crimes who was brought to justice.

In spite of Pearson's arrest, the assaults continued night after horrible night. They were largely attributed to black men, and there were wild theories being thrown around that the Negroes' recent freedom from slavery was to blame. In spite of Austin's generally forward-thinking ways, many white people still thought of African-Americans as uncivilized savages that needed to be tamed, and they felt that the recent string of violent crimes proved their prejudices to be true. But the majority of blame fell squarely on the shoulders of Marshal Grooms Lee.

Lee did what he could to distance himself from responsibility. He insisted that the recent criminal activity was the result of Austin's growing pains and that the transition from cattle town to modern city was not without its price. There was a lot of work to be had in Austin, especially jobs of hard labor, and every day there were new strangers arriving in town, many of them ex-convicts. Houston had recently suffered a similar crime wave, and that had come to an end more or less on its own. Lee was confident that soon enough, the perpetrators of these burglaries, beatings and outrages would simply move on to a new city and become someone else's problem. And by late March, it appeared that he had been right. After months of nightly attacks, things finally seemed to quiet down and the citizens of Austin were treated to a few weeks of relative peace. But by mid-April, everything had started up again, quickly becoming even worse than before. The victims were still predominately black women, but sometimes, German or Swedish girls were attacked as well. The one thing all the victims had in common was that they were all servant girls, usually assaulted in cabins and shanties on their employers' property.

Since the police were proving to be perfectly useless, the newspapers called for residents to arm themselves and form vigilance groups. Perhaps killing off one or two of these midnight marauders might serve as a deterrent to others. There was even a song being sung in the town saloons about the rampage:

> *Get thee a gun, oh serving girl,*
> *And keep it by thy bed,*
> *Take aim upon the ruffian*
> *And fill him full of lead!*

CHAPTER 3: ANOTHER DEED OF DEVILTRY

At six o'clock in the morning of Wednesday, May 6th, 1885, Dr. L.B. Johnson left his home on the corner of Jacinto and Cypress Streets to head to the market, just as he did on most days. Not long after he had left, his wife heard screams coming from the cabin behind their house where their servant, thirty-year-old Eliza Shelley, lived with her three children. Mrs. Johnson sent her young niece out to investigate the source of the screams. The little girl did as her aunt asked and went out to the cabin.

There, she found Eliza lying motionless on the floor, her nightdress pulled up above her waist. Eliza's eight-year-old son was in the corner of the room, screaming and crying while his two younger brothers huddled together on the blood-soaked mattress. Mrs. Johnson's niece went pale with fright, slammed the door shut and ran back to her aunt in hysterics. When the girl finally calmed down enough to report what she had seen, Mrs. Johnson could scarcely believe it and went to the cabin to see the sight herself. Moments later, she also came running back to the house in terror.

When Dr. Johnson returned from the market, he found his wife and niece sitting together in the kitchen, trembling like leaves on a branch. "I believe Eliza's been murdered," Mrs. Johnson said. The doctor dropped everything and hurried out to the cabin where he found that his wife's fears were correct. Eliza was dead. He knelt down next to the body of his longtime servant and examined her. There was a long, deep gash in the woman's head that appeared to have been inflicted with an axe or hatchet. The blow had gone clean through her skull, deep into her brain, and was certainly enough to have killed her, but it wasn't all the woman had suffered. She had also been stabbed above the ear and between the eyes by some long, sharp instrument, perhaps an iron rod.

When Marshal Lee arrived, he found the similarities to the murder of Mollie Smith impossible to ignore. The weapons used in both crimes had been an axe and a metal rod, although this time, neither weapon had been left at the scene. Both women had been attacked in their sleep and both women had been viciously outraged, possibly after they were already dead. This time, however, there had been a witness, albeit a very frightened, confused and distraught eight-year-old boy.

Eliza's son told the police and a Statesman reporter that he woke up in the middle of the night and found a strange man rummaging around the room. When the boy started to cry out, the man told him to be quiet or he would kill him. He then asked the boy where his mother kept her money, to which he replied he didn't know. The man mentioned something about going to St. Louis in the morning, then shoved the boy in the corner, threw a blanket over him and continued his search. After a while, the boy said that he must have fallen back asleep, although Dr. Johnson and Marshal Lee suspected that the intruder had knocked him out with some chloroform that had recently been stolen from a dentist's office. It wasn't until the sun came up that the boy discovered what had become of his mother.

Unfortunately, the child wasn't much help when it came to describing the intruder. He didn't remember if the man was black or white, short or tall, skinny or fat. The only detail he seemed sure of was that the man had been wearing a white bandana over his face.

Dr. Johnson told the police that he would do anything within his power to help them find the killer. Eliza had been working for him for a long time and in many ways, he considered her part of his family. He believed her to be a woman of the utmost character and wanted to see her killer brought to justice. He told Marshal Lee that he couldn't imagine robbery had been the true motive, no matter what the man had said to the little boy. If Eliza had any money at all, it would have only been a few cents she had saved from her wages. She had no jealous ex-lovers, either. Her husband was in prison, and she was totally devoted to him. Neither the Johnsons nor anyone else who had known Eliza had ever seen her in the company of another man, strange or otherwise. In spite of how much he wanted to help, Dr. Johnson could give Lee no names of any suspects to arrest or even question.

The only other clue authorities had to go on was another set of short, broad, bare footprints leading to and from the cabin's door. Old George and the bloodhounds went to work again and again they found nothing helpful. A Sheriff's deputy, however, did happen upon a slow-witted nineteen-year-old black man and arrested him for the simple fact that he wasn't wearing shoes. The footprints did not match his feet, however, and he was quickly released.

Austin's black population was beginning to feel extremely vulnerable. Men were afraid to leave their homes at night out of fear that they might come back and find their wives raped and murdered. The Statesman and other newspapers took full advantage of the public's concerns and printed sensational stories about each and every crime, not sparing a single lurid detail. Austin was a city in the cold grip of fear and no one had any faith in the people who were supposed to protect them.

A week after Eliza's murder, a black man named Ike Plummer was arrested due to the particularly damning testimony of a man named Andrew Rogers. Rogers claimed that on the evening before Eliza had been raped and killed, he had seen Plummer ask her for money. When she refused to give him any, Plummer walked off, shaking his head, muttering that he'd see her again. Rogers also said that he saw what appeared to be the handle of a hatchet sticking out of Plummer's pocket.

Plummer denied every bit of Rogers' story, and even the newspapers that reported it seemed to suggest that the account was a little too convenient to be wholly believed. It was as if Rogers had witnessed everything but the blow that took Eliza Shelley's life. Perhaps he had a vendetta against Plummer or maybe Marshal Lee had given him incentive to create the story out of the need to make a solid arrest. Either way, Plummer was a black man with no solid alibi, so he was held for a while on the circumstantial evidence, although he was ultimately released.

CHAPTER 4: THE SERVANT GIRL ANNIHILATORS

William Sydney Porter, who would later become a famous author of short stories under the pen name O. Henry, was living in Austin in 1885. Not yet able to make a living as a writer, he had come to the city claiming to be looking for work, although by most accounts, the only thing he worked very hard at was avoiding employment. On May 10th, he sent a letter to his friend, Dave Hall, in which he wrote, "Town is fearfully dull except for the frequent raids of the Servant Girl Annihilators, who make things lively in the dull hours of the night." Although the name Porter used to identify the murderer or murderers would not be used again for many years to come, the father of the modern literary twist ending became one of the first people to hang a sensationalized moniker on an unknown serial killer.

Thirteen days after Porter wrote that letter, on the night of May 23rd, a heavy-set, bare-footed black man in a ragged hat and coat entered the two-room apartment of servant girl Irene Cross. As he passed through the first room, Irene's young nephew woke up, saw the intruder and started to scream. The man pulled a knife out of his pocket and told the boy to be quiet, and that he didn't want to have to hurt him. Like Eliza Shelley's son, the boy wisely did as he was told and the man moved into the room where Irene slept.

As he filled the doorway, Irene woke up and immediately started screaming. The man ordered her to shut her mouth and when she didn't, he lunged at her with his knife. Irene's screams of terror transformed into screams of agony as the man sliced the flesh of her arm with a cut so deep and long that it nearly split the limb into two pieces. As torrents of blood streamed out of a severed artery, the man slashed at her again, this time tracing a deep red line halfway around the top of her forehead as if he intended to peel the scalp away from her skull.

Irene's screams had gone on long and loud enough that the man must have thought it best that he make his escape or risk capture. He turned and ran out the way he had entered, through the nephew's room and out the door. Once he was gone, Irene got out of bed and stumbled from the cabin. The noise had awakened her employers, the Whitman family, who came out to the yard and helped the mortally injured woman into the main house.

The police were sent for and so was a doctor, but it was a Statesman reporter who got to the house first. While the Whitmans futilely tried to contain Irene's bleeding, the reporter asked her if she knew who had assaulted her. Having slipped into a state of nearly catatonic shock from the loss of blood and excruciating pain, all Irene was able to do was shake her head no. After getting the details of the story from the woman's nephew, the reporter left to write up his article in time to make it into the morning edition. The doctor did not arrive in time and Irene Cross bled to death, becoming the killer's third victim.

Keeping with the same pattern that had generated no success at all, the hounds were dispatched and several black men found in the area were arrested. Marshal Lee insisted that African-Americans were the focus of the investigation because no white man could possibly have a reason to murder black servant girls, but Austin's black population felt that he might have been using the murders as an excuse to run them out of town.

The arrest of black men had become so common that many resorted to an old slave trick of tying bags of the foul-smelling herb asafetida around their ankles in the hopes of throwing the dogs off their scent.

Again, none of the arrests that were made stuck and the Statesman began criticizing Marshal Lee and his police force even more harshly. Lee came to his own defense with the same excuses he had been using for the past six months. He insisted that the trouble wasn't with his competency or the competency of his men. The problem was that Austin had gotten too big and his police force was too small. How could twelve men be expected to police a town of more than twenty thousand?

CHAPTER 5: AN ATROCIOUS CRIME

As the hot summer months wore on, the killings and even the non-lethal attacks seemed to come to an end and the focus of the citizens of Austin returned to the growth and enrichment of their city. In an effort to reignite a sense of civic pride, cattle baron Jesse Driskill pledged to build the biggest hotel west of the Mississippi right there in the capital city of Texas. On the Fourth of July, the building's cornerstone was laid in a grand ceremony. There were electric lights strung up and down on the streets, a brass band played and champagne was served to all who attended. Mayor John Robertson took the occasion to address the crowd, declaring, "No city in the state has a promise of a more healthful prosperity." But if that promise were to be fulfilled, it would have to wait, because Austin's problems weren't over by a long shot. In fact, the worst was still yet to come.

Rebecca Ramey worked at a livery for the colorfully named Mr. Valentine Weed, roughly a block from Dr. Johnson's house, where Eliza Shelley was murdered back in May. Mr. Weed didn't have a separate servants' cabin on his property, so Rebecca slept in the kitchen of his home with her eleven-year-old daughter, Mary.

On the night of August 30th, Rebecca and Mary went to bed around nine o'clock, just as they always did. Rebecca had trouble falling asleep that night and she lay awake in the darkness for a while. She heard the clock strike ten and then eleven, and drifted off sometime before midnight.

She awoke later in terrible pain, and found herself being tended to by physicians. While she had slept, probably sometime between four and five o'clock in the morning, someone had entered Mr. Weed's kitchen and hit Rebecca in the head so hard that her skull had been fractured. She had been lucky to have survived and was expected to make a full recovery, but that was the only good news of the night. The Servant Girl Annihilator had committed his most vile crime yet, and Rebecca's daughter Mary had been the evening's true victim. After Rebecca had been beaten unconscious, the eleven-year-old girl was dragged into an adjoining washhouse, where she was raped, then stabbed through both ears with a metal rod. The little girl died, although not instantly. She suffered for hours before succumbing to her injuries.

Response to the latest and most horrible attack was swift. The tracker arrived with his bloodhounds before the police even made it to the scene and a furious hunt ensued. A black man named Tom Allen was discovered hiding out in one of Mr. Weed's stables and was arrested immediately. Sticking with the pattern, however, Mr. Allen was found to be innocent and released the very next day. No other suspect was found.

Marshal Lee responded to the public outrage in his usual fashion, but his excuses were wearing thin. The people were demanding action. The rape and murder of an eleven-year-old child was a crime that simply could not be tolerated in a civilized society such as Austin. Someone would have to answer for it and soon.

CHAPTER 6: SLAIN IN THEIR SLEEP

On September 26th, Lucinda Boddy and Patsie Gibson were visiting their friend Gracie Vance in North Austin. Gracie worked for Major W.D. Dunham and lived in a cabin behind the house with her common-law husband, Orange Washington. Foolishly believing their numbers would keep them safe from the criminals who roamed the streets of Austin, they left the window open while they slept so they could enjoy the cool, autumn breeze.

Sometime after midnight, Lucinda woke up with the worst headache she had ever had in her life. She fumbled around in the darkness until she found a kerosene lamp and when she lit it, she saw Orange and Patsie, still lying where they had gone to sleep, but they had grievous wounds to their heads. Her dear friend Gracie was nowhere to be found. Hearing some noises from outside, she took the lamp to the window to investigate.

"Don't look at me!" a man shouted, covering his face with his arm as he rushed towards her, into the light. Lucinda screamed and threw the lamp at him. He batted it away and leaned through the window, trying to grab Lucinda, but she jumped back out of his reach. The man started to climb inside and Lucinda turned and ran through the door on the other side of the room, screaming as loud as she could as she sprinted towards Major Dunham's house.

Awakened by the screams, the major hurried out his back door, armed with his rifle. He saw Lucinda and a shadowy figure struggling at the gate between his house and the servants' cabin. He raised his rifle, but didn't dare take a shot for fear of hitting Lucinda. When the man spotted the major, he released the woman, turned and ran off towards the stables. The major lined up to take his shot, but Lucinda, in her panic, got in his way. "We're all dead!" she screamed, bursting into tears and collapsing into the major's arms as the intruder disappeared into the darkness.

Major Dunham yelled for his neighbors to come out and help him find the man and everyone within earshot responded. A team of armed men spent the rest of the night searching the major's property and the surrounding area with lanterns and torches, but the perpetrator seemed to have vanished. They didn't find the intruder, but they did find the body of his latest victim, Gracie Vance.

It seemed that while Gracie, Lucinda, Patsie and Orange had been sleeping, one or possibly two men climbed in through the open window and beat all four occupants of the cabin unconscious. Gracie was then thrown through the window, tossed over a fence and dragged through the weeds behind the stables. There, she must have regained consciousness, because there were signs of a struggle, but it was a struggle that Gracie lost. She was raped and

beaten with a brick until her head had been re-
duced to jelly.

It was the most daring and violent attack to
date, but this time, the killer or killers seemed
to have finally made a mistake: there were two
clues left behind at the scene. The first was a
saddled horse that did not belong to the major
or any of his neighbors and was found tied to a
tree near the stables. The second was a silver
watch that was found in Gracie's hand. The
chain was wrapped around her wrist as if she
had ripped it off her attacker and he either did
not notice or didn't have time to retrieve it before making his escape. Marshal Lee felt as if
he had finally caught a break. If the horse and
watch could be traced back to their rightful
owners, he might actually end up with a suspect he could hang a conviction on.

But his hopes were quickly dashed. The
horse was discovered to belong to an African-
American man named Beverly Overton, but he
had already reported it stolen. The watch was
also stolen property, rightfully belonging to a
Swedish girl, and another a dead end. It
seemed possible that the watch and horse had

even intentionally been left behind in an effort to send the police off in the wrong direction, maybe even to frame Mr. Overton.

The three survivors were taken to the hospital, where Orange Washington died before the sun came up. Lucinda and Patsie, however, both recovered, and as luck would have it, even though Lucinda didn't get a clear look at the man who nearly killed her, she heard his voice and had recognized it. She told police that the man who attacked her was Gracie Vance's former boyfriend, Dock Woods.

The police tracked Woods down easily enough, and although he insisted on his innocence, he did so while wearing a shirt that was stained with blood. He was immediately arrested along with his brother Doug and a known thief named Oliver Townsend. Doug was released almost immediately, but Dock and Townsend were held as likely suspects. Both men maintained their innocence under questioning, and due to Lucinda's head injury, her identification of Woods' voice was not given much credibility. Lee was unable to get his confessions and his superiors finally felt as if they had no choice but to intervene.

CHAPTER 7: THE NOBLE DETECTIVES

With the escalation of the past two murders and no solid suspects to answer for them, Mayor Robertson put in a call to Houston's Noble Detective Agency and had two men sent to Austin to help Marshal Lee solve these crimes once and for all. When the private detectives arrived in town, they immediately began teaching Marshal Lee and his men some big city tactics on how to coerce confessions out of prisoners. Woods and Townsend were subjected to multiple beatings and degradations, but still, neither one ever confessed to any of the crimes.

In need of a new suspect, Marshal Lee and the Noble detectives turned their attention to Alec Mack, a man who had been an acquaintance of Rebecca Ramey and was known to spend a lot of his time "tramping" in some of the darker corners of Austin's seedier neighborhoods. Mack was a good suspect with his widely known connection to one of the victims and his even more widely known love of spirits.

Lee tracked him down at the Black Elephant, the most popular black saloon in all of Austin. The marshal and detectives escorted Mack out of the bar, assuring him that they only wanted to talk, but the further they walked down the darkened streets, the more ominous and threatening the tone of the meeting became. Mack realized too late that he had made a horrible mistake going off with these men alone. Instead of bringing him to the police station, the lawmen steered him into a dark alley and pushed him up against a wall. Lee told Mack that they knew he was guilty of the murder of Rebecca Ramey and maybe even all the other unsolved murders over the past year and that if he didn't confess, he would soon wish he had. Mack insisted that he had nothing to do with the murders, which, as far as Marshal Lee and the detectives were concerned, was the wrong answer.

They began beating Mack ruthlessly, demanding a confession. Still, he swore he knew nothing about the crimes, even when the men put a rope around his neck. Lee made sure that Mack understood that they weren't bluffing; the days of slavery may have been over, but a black man could still be lynched if he didn't do what white men of authority demanded. But Mack refused to implicate himself, at the same time begging for his life. Just as the detectives were about to lift Mack off the ground, fate intervened in the form of Press Hopkins, a white man who had come out of his house to see what all the ruckus was about. Hopkins ordered Lee and the detectives to stop what they were doing immediately, and they had no choice but to do as they were told.

Mack's life had been saved by Hopkins' timely arrival, but that didn't mean he was free to go. Lee was still convinced they could get a confession out of him, so Mack was taken to the police station where he could be beaten in privacy. Mack suffered at Lee's hands for nine straight days, but he never changed his story. Eventually, the time came when Lee had nothing left to do but let him go. Upon Mack's release, a Statesman reporter couldn't help but notice what terrible condition he was in and interviewed Marshal Lee about his interrogation methods. Lee claimed that Mack had gotten his lumps while resisting arrest, but his story was met with much doubt, especially when word spread about what Press Hopkins had witnessed.

On November 10th, Mayor John Robertson publicly stated, "I have faith that the authors of these crimes will yet be uncovered. No human heart is strong enough to hold such secrets." The mayor's statement may have been seen by most as civic optimism, but Marshal Lee could read the truth between the lines. The mayor was telling him that he was on borrowed time. He had to get a conviction and get one fast. Lee had proven himself incompetent and immoral and unless he put a name to the killer soon, even his father's influence wouldn't be enough to help him keep his job. Out of sheer desperation, Lee turned to the only possible suspect he had left: Walter Spencer.

In early December, almost a full year after the murder that started the whole bloody affair, Lee convinced District Attorney James H. Robertson, the mayor's brother, to try Spencer for Mollie Smith's murder. But with no physical evidence and only a far-fetched theory to present to the court, Spencer was acquitted after two days. As a response, Grooms Lee was relieved of his duties as town marshal and replaced with James Lucy, a former Texas Ranger.

Following Spencer's trial, respected former District Attorney E.T. Moore spoke to the press on his theories about the killer. He believed that the murders were committed by one man with a deep hatred for women, and that the victims were chosen more for what they symbolized rather than for any personal problem the killer had with them. Although Moore had just become one of the first criminal experts in history to profile a serial killer, his ideas were too far ahead of their time. His words were almost exclusively met with derision and summarily dismissed.

CHAPTER 8: BLOOD! BLOOD! BLOOD!

By Christmas Eve of 1885, it had been three months since the attack that claimed the lives of Orange Washington and Gracie Vance. As the people crowded elbow to elbow into church pews that night, many of them were praying for the exact same thing: that the murders of Austin's black servant girls had finally come to an end. And in a sick way worthy of the darkest O. Henry twist, their prayers were answered.

Sometime around eleven o'clock that night, after the night's sermons had concluded and carols had been sung, fifty-year-old Moses Hancock woke up to the sound of distant groans. He was alone in his bed, but that was not unusual, at least not lately. He and his wife, Susan, had been having marital problems and had taken to sleeping in separate rooms. He got up and went through the door to the adjoining room where Susan slept, and saw a sight that had become all too common in Austin that year. The bed was empty and the sheets were drenched in blood. His wife's skirts, also bloodstained, were carelessly discarded on a chair in the corner of the room and a trail of blood led out the door and into the hallway. Hancock grabbed a kerosene lamp and followed the trail outside and around the back of the house. There, he found his wife.

Susan Hancock was still alive, but only barely. She had been struck twice in the head by an axe. One blow had had taken off her ear and crushed her cheekbone, the other split her skull between her ear and eye. Just as with Eliza Shelley and Mary Ramey, some sort of metal rod had been inserted into her brain. Everything about the scene was very familiar, with one notable exception. Susan Hancock was white.

As angry and horrified as the citizens of Austin were during the servant girl murders, the white population had felt relatively secure throughout the year. But the murder of Sue Hancock proved that no one was safe. The killer could strike anyone, anywhere. And the night's escalations weren't over. Less than an hour after Susan Hancock's body was found, there was another murder that shocked Austin all the way to its core.

Eula Phillips, Luly to her friends, was arguably the most beautiful woman in all of Texas. With her milky skin, curly black hair and smoldering eyes, she was the kind of woman men would turn their heads for, even if it meant catching hell from their wives. And it wasn't just her beauty that made her special; one of her grandfathers had been a member of Stephen F. Austin's original colony, which made her as close to royalty as one could get in Texas. She simultaneously represented everything the city had been in the past and everything it had and would become.

But Eula had not lived a life free of hardship. Her mother died while she and her sister Alma were very little and the girls' father, hotelier Thomas Burditt, didn't have any idea how to bring up two young daughters on his own and wouldn't have wanted to even if he had, so he turned the girls to be raised by their aunt.

By December of 1885, Eula was only seventeen, but she was already a wife and a mother. She was married to Jimmy Phillips, a young, handsome musician who was adored by nearly every woman in town. The couple lived with Jimmy's parents at a house on West Hickory Street, one of the wealthiest neighborhoods in all of Austin.

Just before the clock struck midnight, ringing in Christmas Day, Jimmy's mother woke up to the sound of a baby crying. She got out of bed and went across the hall to the room where her son and his family slept. When she opened the door, she was subjected to a terrible, almost surreal sight. Her eighteen-month-old grandson was standing up on the bed, screaming and crying, his nightclothes soaked through with blood, an apple clutched in his

tiny hands. It was all too much for Mrs. Phillips
to process and she fainted. When she recovered moments later, she found herself staring
at a bloody axe that had been discarded in the
middle of the bedroom floor.

She got to her feet and scooped the child
up in her arms. He was unhurt; thankfully the
blood was not his. At least some of it, however,
belonged to Mrs. Phillips' son. Jimmy was in
bed, barely conscious, a horrible, bloody gash
on the back of his head and neck. Eula was nowhere to be found, but her pillow had even
more blood on it than the one under Jimmy's
head. Once again, a trail of blood begged to
be followed. It led out onto the porch where a
bloody footprint was also found, then continued through the backyard to a narrow alley,
where it came to a grisly end.

The beautiful young Eula Phillips, the pride
of Austin, had been dead for roughly half an
hour, her forehead caved in by a terrible blow.
She was laid out completely naked and spread
eagle, heavy pieces of lumber placed over her
wrists as if meant to keep her in place. The
killer had placed her on display. The reporters

who managed to get a glimpse of her body before it was moved claimed that the expression on her face indicated that she had died in intense agony.

The next morning, the Austin Daily Statesman screamed out: "Blood! Blood! Blood!" and "The Demons Have Transferred Their Thirst for Blood to White People!" The usual Christmas Day festivities were cancelled and instead, a thousand of Austin's citizens gathered at the Hall of Representatives to discuss what should be done.

While there had been talk of forming vigilance committees earlier in the year, the city's most prominent men were suddenly inspired to provide the funding to make them into a reality. A curfew was put into effect and it was ordered that saloons and brothels would have to cease their all-night operations and close their doors at midnight. Additionally, there would be a zero tolerance policy towards strangers in town. The sheriff and his deputies were instructed by Marshal Lucy to question each and every man they didn't personally know, and if someone didn't have a damn good reason for being there, he would be given twenty-four hours to get the hell out. The wealthiest businessmen in town collectively put up a $3,000 reward and the governor himself put up $300 for the killer's capture. By the end of Christmas Day there had been multiple arrests, including six black men, one mentally ill Mexican-American and two white brothers who were found with blood on their clothes one town north. None of them turned out to be solid suspects, however, and all were eventually released.

Over the next few weeks, Austin practically became a police state. Nearly every bounty hunter and private detective in Texas had found his way to town. The sale of guns increased like never before, and those who could afford them purchased newfangled security devices such as "electric burglar alarms" like the ones they used up in New York City. Reporters came from all over to cover the story. All eyes of the country were on Austin.

D.A. Robertson was under incredible pressure. After the embarrassing affair that was the trial of Walter Spencer and with the sacking of Grooms Lee, Robertson had become the town's newest scapegoat. He needed a conviction.

As he searched desperately for a suspect, one thought kept occurring to him. Perhaps the white women weren't killed by the same man who had murdered all those black servant girls at all. Maybe their killer or killers only wanted the world to think they had been. Maybe the murders had been staged to look like they were part of the spree, but Eula and Susan were killed for different reasons altogether. It didn't take him long to decide what those reasons must have been, and in January of 1886, Jimmy Phillips and Moses Hancock were arrested for the murders of their wives.

CHAPTER 9: NATHAN ELGIN

Dick Rogers ran a saloon in East Austin, which meant he was no stranger to trouble. When men got drunk, they sometimes got violent and that was just the way of things, especially in the poorer parts of town. Dick knew better than to get involved in other men's quarrels most of the time, other than to suggest they settle their disagreements outside the walls of his fine establishment, but the night of February 8th, 1886 tested his limits.

A young man named Nathan Elgin had been buying drinks for a girl named Julia all night long. When they had both gotten sufficiently drunk, Elgin suggested that they go somewhere where they could be alone and get to know each other a little better. Julia turned him down and Elgin had responded by smacking the girl down to the floor. He then proceeded to beat on her with such rage that no one in the saloon dared to intervene past yelling for him to stop. But Elgin didn't stop. He grabbed Julia by the hair and dragged her out of the saloon.

Dick Rogers had no choice but to send for the police, even though it was always dangerous when the law had to come to East Austin. With all the arrests that had been made over the past year, a white lawman coming into a crowd of drunken black men was going to be was a recipe for disaster. But Elgin had to be stopped before he seriously hurt that poor girl or worse. While waiting for the police to arrive, Rogers and some of his patrons followed Elgin two blocks down the street, where he dragged Julia into a house and continued inflicting his punishment. Elgin had already beaten the girl bloody, and now he was going to rape her, maybe even kill her.

By the time Officer John Bracken arrived on the scene, it seemed as if the entire neighborhood had come out on the streets to see what was going on. He asked the crowd for help in subduing Elgin, and Rogers volunteered, as did a neighborhood man named Claibe Hawkins. The three men went into the house and found Elgin still beating on Julia. Rogers and Hawkins rushed up and grabbed him from behind. They tried to wrestle his arms behind his back so Bracken could cuff him, but Elgin managed to wrench himself free. He then pulled a knife and brandished it at the officer. Rogers and Hawkins backed off and Bracken tried to talk Elgin into surrendering, but Elgin wasn't in the mood to talk. He was in the mood to fight. The struggle took them back outside, into the crowd, where Elgin knocked Bracken off his feet. Suddenly, a gunshot rang out. Someone in the crowd had fired at Bracken. Whether he thought it was Elgin who had shot at him, or whether it was just the excuse he needed to put an end to the matter, Officer Bracken drew his own pistol and fired. Nathan Elgin went down and never got up again.

This wasn't Elgin's first run-in with the law. He had a history of fighting authority, especially when he had been drinking. In 1881, he had been involved in a gunfight near the governor's mansion and in 1882, he had sent a letter to a sheriff's deputy, threatening to kill him the next time they met. He was nineteen years old, and already a husband and father of two children, although he didn't live with his family. He worked as a cook in a downtown restaurant, and he lived there, too. His wife, Sallie, lived with their children at a white family's residence, where she worked as a servant girl.

For a few days after he was shot, Elgin clung stubbornly to life. Bracken's bullet had struck him in the spine, paralyzing him. While he was being treated, the doctors made an interesting discovery: Elgin only had four toes on his right foot. There were few men in town that knew just how significant that fact truly was.

Over a year ago, when Mollie Smith was found murdered, what followed was a private inquest, and the press questioned what details were being kept from the public's knowledge. One such detail was that the bare footprint that was found at the scene only had four toes. All of a sudden, the police had a solid suspect for the eight unsolved murders of the past year. But Elgin never confessed and refused to answer any questions at all until he finally succumbed to his injuries and died.

It seemed as if Nathan Elgin were the true murderer and justice had ultimately been done. However, there are other accounts of the night he was shot that cast doubt on this theory. There are some who claim that the girl Julia didn't exist at all, and that the woman Elgin was dragging from the saloon was his wife, Sallie, who had gotten very drunk and was making a scene. When Bracken showed up to arrest him, the people of the neighborhood tried to protect him from the officer, but Bracken managed to shoot Elgin in the back. The police then concocted a story to protect Bracken and the rest of the force, and decided to pin the servant girl murders on him for good measure. After all, the statement that the killer had a four-toed right foot could have been invented after Elgin had died or Elgin's toe could have been removed after he had been paralyzed. The truth will most likely never be known, but one thing is certain. After Elgin's death, the murders stopped completely. There was never another murder of a black servant girl or a rich white woman or anyone in between that fit the pattern of the killing spree.

And even if Elgin had committed the murders of Mollie Smith, Eliza Shelley, Irene Cross, Mary Ramey, Orange Washington and Gracie Vance, it didn't change D.A. Robertson's theory. He still believed that Eula Phillips and Susan Hancock were killed by their own husbands and very soon, he would prove it in court.

CHAPTER 10: TRIAL OF THE CENTURY

The trial of Jimmy Phillips took place at the Travis County Courthouse, and the building was packed to capacity every single day. Robertson had called on his predecessor, E.T. Moore, whose recent theories about the killer had been ridiculed, to aid in the prosecution. They would be facing off against the defense's dream team of William Walton and John Hancock, the best lawyers Jimmy's father could buy.

Even in spite of the terrible wound he received on the night of Eula's murder, Jimmy was a good suspect for the prosecution. On the surface, he and his young wife had been a happy, perfect couple. But it quickly came out in court how deceiving appearances could truly be. The more witnesses that were brought forward, the more secrets and lies were exposed.

It became evident that Eula had never really been happy in the marriage. Jimmy was a heavy drinker, and a mean drunk. It was well known among the family's close friends and acquaintances that he had been abusive towards her. It was said that on more than one occasion, Jimmy had thrown things at her and had even chased her with a knife. One time, he had scared Eula so badly that she had hidden out at her sister Alma's house for days. One of her friends testified that when she became pregnant with her second child, Eula had ingested a combination of chamomile flowers, extract of cottonwood and ergot to induce a miscarriage. No one in town could believe that this beautiful, wealthy young couple had such darkness in their relationship.

But it was what Eula had been doing the past several months that was most shocking of all. Eula had been frequenting May Tobin's house of assignation on Congress Avenue. It was a well-known but largely unspoken fact that Tobin's place of business was a house where lovers met to cheat on their spouses and where men of power and wealth could discreetly visit high-priced prostitutes. It wasn't simply another brothel or bordello; it was a place that specialized in secrets. Eula Phillips had been there about half a dozen times in the fall of 1885 and May Tobin testified in court that she had even been there on Christmas Eve, only an hour or so before she was found murdered. She had come by with a man in a carriage whose face Tobin claimed she never saw. Christmas Eve was one of Ms. Tobin's busiest times of the year and she didn't have any rooms available, so she had to turn Eula and her companion away.

There was speculation that maybe Eula had fallen in love with someone else and that was the reason for her frequent trips to the house of assignation, but it is more widely believed that she was working as a prostitute in an effort to save up enough money so that she and her son could leave her abusive husband and start a new life in another town. Before the trial, May Tobin told the prosecution that Eula's clients included some of the most prominent businessmen and politicians in Austin. William J. Swain, the state comptroller, was one of the names Tobin named. Swain was a shoo-in for governor in the next election and the press had a field day with the allegations. Swain denied everything and accused his main rival for the seat, Sul Ross, of being behind the rumors, but the damage was done. Even though Tobin didn't mention Swain's name when she testified in court, when the elections were held later that year, Ross defeated his much more handsome, charismatic and publicly disgraced opponent.

When Ms. Tobin took the witness stand, she identified four men whom she had seen with Eula. Two were young politicians, one of whom was secretary of the committee overseeing the building of the new state capitol building, and the other was head of the state public education department. She also implied that she could have named more names, but was being paid to keep silent. Jimmy's sister, Delia, was supposed to back up Ms. Tobin's testimony, but she had been paid to leave town during the trial so that she wouldn't be able to report what she knew of Eula's affairs.

Although there was no firm proof that Jimmy had any prior knowledge of Eula's infidelities, D.A. Robertson argued to the jury that he must have found out about them and that Eula knew that he knew, so she had brought the axe into the room for her own protection. They speculated that Jimmy had found the axe, become enraged and attacked her with it, but not before she had managed to hit him in the back of the head first. Then, after he had killed her, he dragged her out into the alley and staged her body to make her look like the victim of the murderer of the black servant girls. It was an outrageous theory with little basis in fact, but due to all the shocking testimony, it was one the jury was inclined to believe.

Throughout the trial, circumstantial evidence and idle speculation kept coming. A police sergeant testified for the prosecution that when one of the hounds sniffed Eula's body, it turned, ran into the house and reared up on Jimmy, who was still in his bed, being treated for his injuries. John Hancock, one of Jimmy's high-priced lawyers, objected, saying, "I wouldn't hang a dog upon such testimony of a dog!"

Still, the jury was clearly on the side of the prosecution, and Robertson and Moore just had to deal with the bloody footprint found on the porch to nail the case shut. The footprint showed definite similarities to the prints found at the other crime scenes, but it was inconclusive whether the person who had left it was missing a toe on his right foot. Jimmy's lawyers had him place his bare foot in ink and a comparison was made, clearly showing that Jimmy's foot was much smaller. The prosecution's E.T. Moore argued that the weight of Eula's body would cause Mr. Phillips' foot to spread out and become larger, so to settle the matter, a juror suggested that they measure Jimmy's foot again, but this time while holding the weight of another person. Walton agreed and climbed onto Jimmy's back. Hunched over with his own lawyer's arms around his neck and legs around his waist, Jimmy stepped in the ink again, and again his footprint was compared against the one found on the porch. Again, it was found to be too small.

It was quite a trial featuring scandalous, shocking testimony and outrageous courtroom antics. And although no solid physical evidence was ever introduced to implicate Jimmy Phillips in the death of his wife, the jury found him guilty of murder in the second degree and he was sentenced to seven years in prison.

Next came the trial of Moses Hancock. Hancock was not nearly as wealthy as Phillips, but one of Jimmy's lawyers, John Hancock (no relation) represented him pro bono. The most significant piece of evidence the prosecution had against Hancock was a letter that had been found under some fake flowers in a trunk in his wife Susan's room. The letter she had written stated that although she still loved her husband very much, she couldn't live with his drinking anymore and was going to leave him. The D.A. suggested that Moses had read the letter, then gotten drunk and murdered Susan in a rage. It seemed odd that two men would decide on the same night to kill their wives and blame their deaths on the murderer of black servant girls, but that was what the D.A. asked the jury to believe. However, the prosecution's case fell apart when Hancock's teenage daughter testified that her mother had never shown her father the letter she had written. The jury was unable to agree on a verdict and Moses Hancock was released.

Six months later, the Texas Court of Appeals overturned the Phillips verdict due to lack of evidence. The court decided that the testimony of Eula's infidelity should not have been allowed since the prosecution couldn't prove that Jimmy knew about it.

New trials were ordered for both Phillips and Hancock, but neither ever happened.

Eventually, both men left Austin and never came back. Phillips left his and Eula's son with his sister and moved to Georgetown, where he got a job at a chair factory, remarried and fathered a new family. He never spoke of the events of Christmas Eve, 1885 or the trial that followed, but he complained about headaches for the rest of his life and continued to be a scary, volatile man when he was drunk until his death in 1929 at the age of sixty-eight.

Epilogue: A Killer's Legacy

On August 31st, 1888, sometime between the hours of too late and too early, Mary Ann Nichols, known around London, England as "Polly," was seen standing on the corner of Osborn Street and Whitechapel Road, trying to earn enough money to rent a bed for the night. At 3:30 a.m., she was found lying on the street, her skirts raised, her throat and abdomen slashed with a knife. In life, Polly was known as little more than a drunk and a cheap prostitute, but in death, she would become known as the first victim of the most famous unidentified serial killer of all time, Jack the Ripper.

Although Red Jack's murders occurred an ocean away and nearly three years later, there are many historians and amateur sleuths who believe he and the Servant Girl Annihilator were the same man. The strongest suspect linking the two sets of crimes is a Malay cook known as Maurice, who was in Austin in 1885, working at a small hotel called the Pearl House, only blocks from where the murders of Susan Hancock, Mary Ramey and Eliza Shelley were committed. Maurice left Austin in January of 1886, shortly after the deaths of Susan Hancock and Eula Phillips, and was reported to have been in London at the time of the Whitechapel murders.

Maybe Maurice began scratching his itch to kill on the poor black servant girls of Austin because they were such easy targets. Maybe he knew he would be leaving town and felt that shifting his rage towards white women was a risk he was willing to take on that horrible Christmas Eve in 1885. If the testimony at Jimmy Phillips' trial is to be believed, Eula was a part-time prostitute, and it's a well-known fact that the ladies of the night were Jack the Ripper's favorite targets.

But the connection between the two early serial killers is little more than speculation. No one knows for sure who committed the eight murders in Austin between New Year's Eve of 1884 and Christmas Eve of 1885 and it's highly unlikely that anyone ever will. For many years, the crimes themselves seemed to have been more or less written out of the history books until a small mention of them was stumbled upon by novelist Steven Saylor. After digging up the buried tale, Saylor penned the historical fiction novel, A Twist at the End, in which he imagines the author O. Henry in the thick of the intrigue. Later, the crimes were explored in a more factual light, most notably by Skip Hollandsworth in an article for the magazine Texas Monthly, and J.R. Galloway, who painstakingly compiled virtually every newspaper article linked to the crimes in his book, The Servant Girl Murders: Austin, Texas 1885.

There are plenty of theories and wild guesses as to who terrorized the city of Austin for one bloody year towards the end of the nineteenth century. Maybe the killer was the four-toed drunk, Nathan Elgin. Maybe it was Maurice the Malay cook, who possibly went on to commit a more famous series of murders. Maybe it was even Eula Phillips' most esteemed alleged client, Comptroller Swain, as some have speculated. Maybe the same man committed all eight murders, maybe it was a team of criminals, or maybe all but one or two were completely unrelated. The truth is lost to the ages. The identity of the Servant Girl Annihilator remains an American mystery.

REFERENCE

Galloway, J.R., The Servant Girl Murders: Austin, Texas 1885, 2010.

Hollandsworth, Skip, "Capital Murders," Texas Monthly, July, 2000.

Saylor, Steven, A Twist at the End, Simon & Schuster, 2000.

http://en.wikipedia.org/wiki/Servant_Girl_Annihilator

http://www.trutv.com/library/crime/serial_killers/history/servant_girl/index.html

http://www.texasmonthly.com/content/capital-murder

http://www.casebook.org/dissertations/dst-austin.html?printer=true

http://photos1.blogger.com/blogger/1068/1741/1600/crop0018.jpg

http://www.hlntv.com/article/2013/02/12/when-serial-killers-strike-austin-servant-girl-annihilator-murders

http://www.amazon.com/Twist-End-Novel-Henry/dp/0684856816/ref=sr_1_1?ie=UTF8&qid=1311899162&sr=8-1

http://www.fictionpress.com/s/1244843/1/A-Twist-on-a-Twist

http://www.servantgirlmurders.com/

http://en.wikipedia.org/wiki/Mary_Ann_Nichols

http://www.websleuths.com/forums/archive/index.php/t-91056.html

http://jayssouth.com/texas/killer/

http://www.examiner.com/article/the-hush-hush-history-of-the-moonlight-towers

http://www.scribd.com/doc/84313816/The-Mammoth-Book-of-Killers-at-Large-Nigel-Cawthorne

http://query.nytimes.com/mem/archive-free/pdf?res=9E03E2D8123FE533A25755C2A9649D94649FD7CF

http://murders.betterwholeness.com/servant-girl.html

http://books.google.com/books?id=ayHr0mFX6LYC&pg=PA555&lpg=PA555&dq=walter+spencer+mollie+smith&source=bl&ots=rr--x-8tt3&sig=F2Cfsoy1q8lXDUeg-gjPeHAjlYl&hl=en&sa=X&ei=N0U2UZbRJOb-gyQG34YHwAQ&ved=0CDcQ6AEwAjgK#v=onepage&q=walter%20spencer%20mollie%20smith&f=false

http://wagnerfilm.blogspot.com/2006/02/anni-hilator-first-murder.html

http://www.austinchronicle.com/features/2001-01-26/80326/

http://womenincrimeink.blog-spot.com/2009/12/christmas-tidings-of-may-hem.html

http://query.nytimes.com/mem/archive-free/pdf?res=F60A1EF9345C15738DDDAE089 4D8415B8884F0D3

http://en.wikipedia.org/wiki/James_Maybrick

http://www.casebook.org/press_re-ports/atchison_daily_globe/881119.html

http://en.wikipe-dia.org/wiki/Talk%3AServant_Girl_Annihila-tor#Suspect_Nathan_Elgin

http://www.bookofodds.com/Relationships-Society/Crime-Punishment/Articles/A0575-An-Unsolved-Serial-Killing

http://www.casebook.org/forum/messages/4927/5554.html

http://whatwasthen.blogspot.com/2011/08/servant-girl-annihilator.html

http://en.wikipedia.org/wiki/Moonlight_tower

READY FOR MORE?

We hope you enjoyed reading this series. If you are ready to read similar stories, check out other books in the *Cold Case Crimes* series:

Jeff Davis 8: The True Story Behind the Unsolved Murder That Allegedly Inspired True Detective, Season One (By Fergus Mason)

Jefferson Davis Parish has been described as quaint, and in many ways it certainly is. For anyone from a big city much of the area, especially out among the farms, is like a trip in a time machine. For a sleepy rural community, however, Jefferson Davis is a lot more violent than you'd expect, and these days cheap, potent rocks of cocaine are at the root of a lot of that violence.

Crack addicts are famously willing to do just about anything to subsidize their habit so street prostitution has become a real issue, mostly concentrated in the town's poorer neighborhoods south of the railway track. Prostitution – especially on the street – is a dangerous business, so the sheriff's office weren't too surprised when the first one turned up dead. As the body count climbed people started to take notice, but despite all their efforts the killings continued until eight women were dead.

This book traces one of the most fascinating unsolved crimes in the history of Louisiana. In 2014, many believe it became one of the inspirations for the first season of HBO's "True Detective." But the crimes in this book are much more shocking than anything captured on TV.

The Martyr of El Salvador: The Assassination of Óscar Romero (By Reagan Martin)

Óscar Romero, a respected Catholic priest, called on soldiers, as Christians, to put down their arms and stop carrying out the governments order to strip citizens of the most basic human rights...for this he was assassinated. For over 30 years, his murder has gone unsolved.

Who would murder a priest who only wanted to stop the injustice? And more importantly, why is it that, with substantial evidence naming the murderers involved, was nothing done to convict those guilty of murdering the country's beloved archbishop?

The Axeman: The Brutal History of the Axeman of New Orleans (By Wallace Edwards)

Between 1918 to 1919 a serial killer ran rampant throughout New Orleans. His weapon of choice? The axe. He didn't spare women. Or children. Or even men. There was only one kind of person who could be sparred from the blade of his axe: the home of a person playing jazz music. At least eight people were brutally murdered. Who could have been responsible for this crime, and how was the Mafia connected? Did a corrupt police department intentionally leave this case unsolved?

Come, if you dare, as Absolute Crime takes you on the hunt for one of the most brutal killers who ever lived.

The Galapagos Murder: The Murder Mystery That Rocked the Equator (By Fergus Mason)

The Galapagos Islands are a scientist's haven. Home to rare creatures, it was made famous by Charles Darwin and is the ideal spot for study, relaxation...and murder?

In September 1929 two settlers arrived on the desolate island of Floreana. They dreamed of escaping it all and were living the dream, until an arrogant Baroness and her lovers arrived. Turning an island paradise into a living hell, the Baroness suddenly disappeared without a trace. To this day, no one is sure what happened to her.

This is the story of love, paradise, betrayal, and murder. It will have you thinking twice before you ever yearn to escape to your own tropical paradise!

Young, Queer, and Dead: A Biography of San Francisco's Most Overlooked Serial Killer, The Doodler (By Reagan Martin)

The Zodiac Killer may have been San Francisco's most notorious serial killer, but another equally cruel killer was also stalking the streets at the same time, and, just like the Zodiac Killer, has never been arrested for his crimes. The difference is, while the Zodiac Killer's murder spree was heavily publicized, this other killer, nicknamed The Doodler, went unreported by the media and is nearly unknown today.

How did this ruthless killer become almost forgotten? Because he didn't target helpless women or children--he targeted gays--and in the 70s many people believed they had it coming; if they would just stop being gay, then all would be well.

In this gripping short book, you will go on the trail for one of the most brutal killers who ever lived. Read about why his victims were disregarded by a homophobic press, and how he was positively identified by three escaped victims...only to walk away free without being arrested.

Getting Away With Murder: 15 Chilling Cold Cases That Will Make You Think Twice About Going Outside (By William Webb)

Despite a decline in the number of murders in the United States since the 1960s, thousands go unsolved each year. As of 2013, the solve rate was at an all time low at only 65 percent of the total committed.

The 15 murders profiled in this book were committed between 1958 and 2014. The oldest of the set involves the bizarre murder of Pearl Eaton, one of the famous Ziegfeld Follies Girls of the 1920s. From the beginning, the crime had no leads or suspects and remains among the coldest of the 15 unsolved crimes. The most recent – the murder of four members of the McStay family found buried in the California desert in November 2013 – is under active investigation.

NEWSLETTER OFFER

Don't forget to sign up for your newsletter to grab your free book:

http://www.absolutecrime.com/newsletter

www.ingramcontent.com/pod-product-compliance
Lightning Source LLC
Chambersburg PA
CBHW020300030426
42336CB00010B/845